CLIL Readers

 Audio available

The healthy food party

written by
Amy White

illustrated
by Mima Castro

Richmond

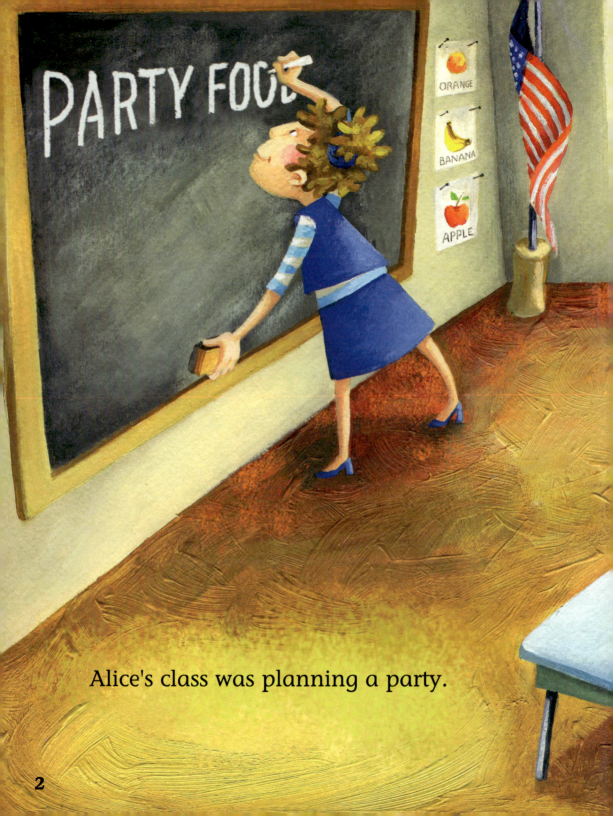

Alice's class was planning a party.

'Let's have sweets!' John said.
'I want lots of chips!' said Fred.

Miranda wanted chips too. Janie wanted pies. Alex asked for cake. Anna asked for lemonade.

'We need healthy food,' said Alice.
'Too much junk food is not good for you.'

The children all raised their hands.
They just did not understand.

'Don't worry,' said Alice.
'I know just what to do.'

Then, Alice looked around.
Her eyes lit up at what she found.

'This chart shows healthy food,' said Alice. 'Healthy food is good for you.'

Then, she sang the *Healthy Food Song*:
'Healthy food is good to eat.
It keeps you strong from head to feet.'

10

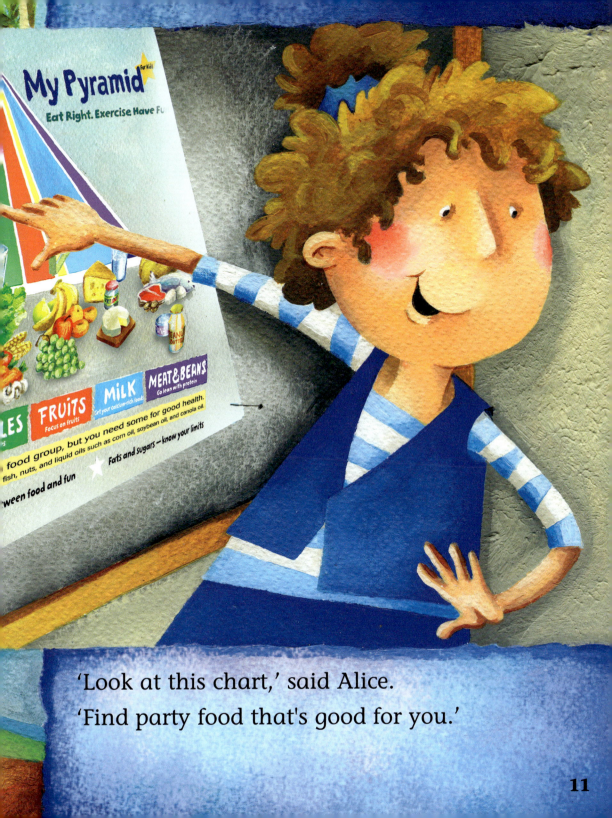

'Look at this chart,' said Alice.
'Find party food that's good for you.'

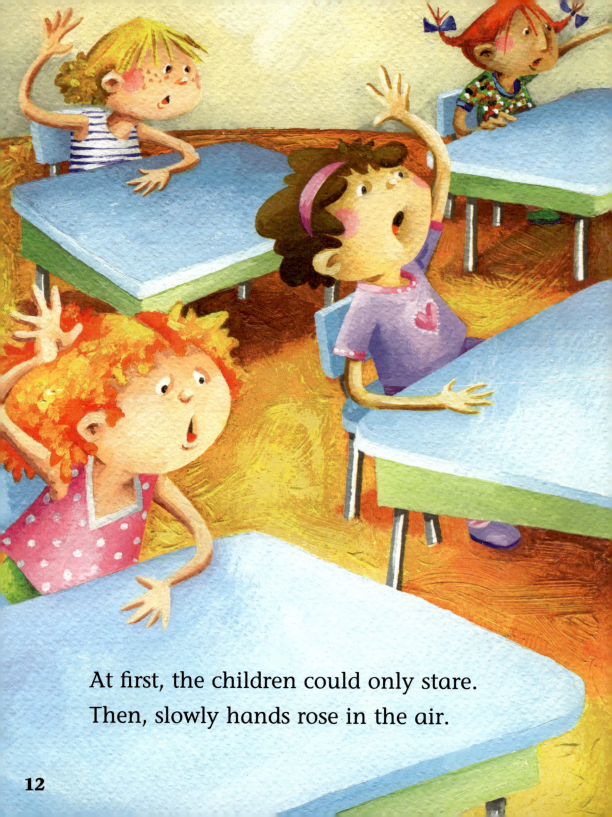

At first, the children could only stare.
Then, slowly hands rose in the air.

'I like bananas,' said Hannah.
'I like juice,' said Elisabeth.

'Can we have steak?' asked Jake.
'Can we have ham?' asked Pam.

'I'll bring a tomato,' said Rita.
'I'll bring cheese,' said Louise.

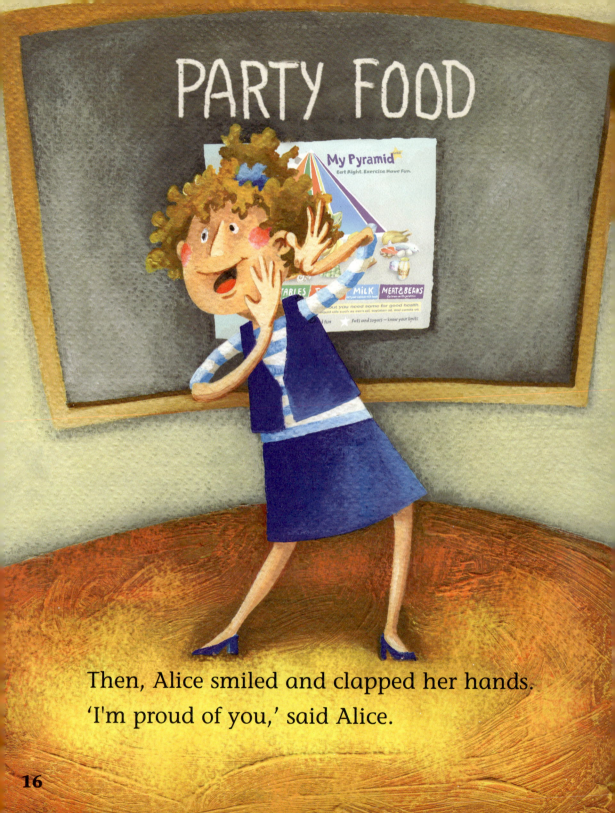

Then, Alice smiled and clapped her hands. 'I'm proud of you,' said Alice.